Alaska's Glaciers

Frozen in Motion

by Katherine Hocker

Alaska Geographic would like to thank the following experts for their careful review of *Frozen in Motion* as it was developed: Bruce A. Giffen, Geologist, National Park Service; James F. Baichtal, Forest Geologist, Tongass National Forest; Lezlie Murray, Manager, Begich Boggs Visitor Center; and Joanna Hubbard, Science Specialist, Anchorage School District.

Author: Katherine Hocker

Illustrations/Maps: Kathy Lepley

Graphic Design: Chris Byrd, Debbie Whitecar

Managing Editor: Jill Brubaker

Project Coordinator: Lisa Oakley

Photography: ©Ron Niebrugge/wildnatureimages.com Backcover, 10, 11UL, 14UL, 15UR, 28, 35LL, 35LR, 36, 44UL, 51, 14UL; ©Michael Collier 4, 15LL, 15LR, 17, 18, 24, 32, 35UL, 42-43, 44LR, 45UL; ©Fred Hirschmann 11UL, 14UR, 22UL, 22LR, 30, 34, 40; ©2006 Jeff Schultz/AlaskaStock.com 6; ©2006 David Job/AlaskaStock.com 14L; ©2006 Jeff Schultz/AlaskaStock.com 23; ©2006 Mark Kelley/AlaskaStock.com 11; ©2006 David Job/AlaskaStock.com 20; ©2006 Mark kelley/AlaskaStock.com 27; ©2006 David Job/AlaskaStock.com 48; ©2006 Mark Kelley/AlaskaStock.com 39;Clara Rust Collection, 67-110-508, Archives, Alaska and Polar Regions Collections, Rasmuson Library, University of Alaska Fairbanks 29; Chris Byrd 12; Katherine Hocker 45 LR; David Job 35UR, 46, 49; Roy Wood 9.

(U=upper part of page, L=lower part of page, R=on the right, L=one the left)

Alaska Geographic is a nonprofit publisher of books and other materials about Alaska's public lands. For more information or to join visit www.alaskageographic.org

Alaska
Geographic

241 North C Street
Anchorage, AK 99501
www.alaskageographic.org

ISBN-13: 978-0-930931-76-6

Library of Congress Cataloging-in-Publication Data
Hocker, Katherine M.
Frozen in motion : Alaska's glaciers / by Katherine Hocker.
p. cm.
Summary: "Introduction to the geology of glaciers in Alaska. Includes glossary and hands-on learning activities"--Provided by publisher.
ISBN 0-930931-76-9
1. Glaciers--Alaska--Juvenile literature. 2. Geology--Study and teaching--Activity programs--Alaska--Juvenile literature. I. Title.
GB2425.A4H63 2005
551.31'2'09798--dc22
2005018582

Printed in China on recycled paper.

Contents

Malaspina Glacier – Wrangell-St. Elias National Park & Preserve

Frozen in Motion—Alaska's Glaciers

What does a glacier look like?
A glacier is white, and blue as deep water, and as dirty as a gravel hill, and clear as a windowpane. It is smooth as whipped cream and as wrinkled as a crumpled piece of paper. It has bands and stripes and swirls.

There are glaciers in many areas of the world—in Europe, Asia, North America, South America, and even Africa. Greenland and Antarctica are almost completely covered by glaciers. But the glaciers of Alaska are particularly abundant, active, and fascinating. Scientists come from all over the world to study their "frozen motion," and travelers come from all over the world to visit them.

What does a glacier sound like?
A glacier rumbles and roars, and chimes and pings. It crackles and fizzes. It creaks and moans and thumps.

What does a glacier feel like?
A glacier is cold and solid, scalloped and sharp. It's sticky and slippery, rough and grainy and smooth.

What is a glacier?
A glacier is a huge mass of ice that flows downhill. It's powerful enough to carry mountains to the sea, but it can disappear with warming climate. It's a rock-breaker and a river-maker.

Portage Valley – Chugach National Forest

1

A Land of Glaciers—Where Glaciers Are Found in Alaska

It's 10 p.m., but the sun is still shining on the snow-covered peaks around your Alaska campsite. Sunset won't be for another hour at least. Swainson's thrushes and orange-crowned warblers chime sweet songs in the nearby willows.

You turn to the east, where a glacier spills from the mountains to the valley floor. Its white surface is crisscrossed with deep blue crevasses that seem to swallow the evening light. As you watch, a piece of ice breaks off of its face and tumbles to the rocks below. A few moments later, you hear the crash, and its echoes.

Something rustles in the brush near where the ice fell. Through your binoculars, you see a moose looking up, startled, with leaves caught in his antlers. The sound of the falling ice has interrupted his dinner. After a moment he goes back to munching on willow. He's used to that sound, after all—he's lived most of his life in the shadows of Alaska's glaciers.

Alaska is famous for its spectacular scenery: tall waterfalls, rugged peaks, soaring cliffs, and mirrored lakes. Most of this beautiful landscape was created by thousands of glaciers, over thousands of years.

Want to Visit a Glacier?

1. ***Mendenhall Glacier,*** in the **Tongass National Forest**, is about fifteen miles from downtown Juneau, at the head of a valley where thousands of people live. For the best views, stop in at the forest service visitor center and then go for a hike on one of the many trails that take you within just a short distance of the glacier's face. You can even wade with the icebergs in Mendenhall Lake (BRRR…)

2. ***Glacier Bay National Park*** is an enormous series of bays in Southeast Alaska. In 1794, explorer George Vancouver found what is now ***Glacier Bay*** completely filled in by a single glacier that has since melted back and separated into twelve smaller ones. There's a visitor center near the mouth of the bay, but to see glaciers and icebergs, take a tour boat, a floatplane, or a kayak 60 miles up the bay.

3. ***Worthington Glacier State Recreation Site*** is on your way between Glennallen and Valdez. There, you'll find an interpretive trail, and also a one-mile hike along the rocky top of a moraine (a pile of rubble left behind when the glacier melted) that takes you up to a great view of the upper surface of the ice.

4. ***Portage Glacier,*** fifty-five miles south of Anchorage, used to be visible from the Begich, Boggs Visitor Center on the shore of Portage Lake. Like a shy animal, it has retreated back around the corner of a mountain. To see its face, you'll need to take a boat trip. But there are still plenty of icebergs in the lake, and you can often find one close to the visitor center.

5. ***Kenai Fjords National Park*** near Seward has many active tidewater glaciers easily seen by boat. Or visit ***Exit Glacier,*** just a short drive out of Seward, where you'll find rangers, a nature center, and many trails to take you close to the glacier's face or along its side.

6. ***Muldrow Glacier*** lies in the heart of ***Denali National Park and Preserve,*** and is easy to see from the Eielson Visitor Center. Look sharp, though, because you might not recognize the glacier at first… it's covered with debris, and even has trees growing on some parts of it.

7. ***Matanuska Glacier*** can be seen from mile 101 on the Glenn Highway, about 100 miles north of Anchorage. Like all glaciers, the Matanuska is constantly changing. In the twentieth century, it advanced and receded several times.

On June 6, 1912, a massive, three-day long eruption caused Mount Katmai to collapse inward on itself, creating a caldera (or crater). As snow fell and settled into the newly exposed bowl, a glacier was born. Today, there are two glaciers inside the volcanic crater that extend from the rim to the edge of a crater lake, which coninues to slowly fill the caldera. The **Katmai Caldera Glaciers** are among a very few glaciers in the world with a known birth date because they could not have existed before the volcanic eruption.

Glacier Safety

Glaciers are beautiful, and they're fun to explore, but explore them safely. Never approach a glacier's face or climb on a glacier unless you're with an experienced glacier guide. When hiking in glacier country, dress warmly. Be careful near icebergs—they can roll over, or drop pieces of ice, at any time.

Exit Glacier – Kenai National Park

There are more glaciers in Alaska than anywhere else in the United States. Because many Alaska glaciers are interconnected into icefields, it's hard to give a total number for sure. By most estimates, there are approximately one hundred thousand glaciers in Alaska.

That probably doesn't surprise anyone. Alaska is famous for snow and ice, especially in the frigid arctic zone in the far north of the state. So the Arctic must be where most of the glaciers are, right?

Actually, no. In fact, there are very few glaciers north of the Alaska Range (in the center of the state). Glacier ice forms in places where lots of snow falls each winter, and where winter snow stays through the summer. The arctic environment is just too dry, and its summers are too warm, for enough snow to accumulate.

The mountains along the southern coast are the heart of Alaska's glacier country. In the Chugach, Wrangell, St. Elias, Kenai, and Coast mountains, each winter can dump 100 feet or more of snow (that's enough to bury an eight-story building!). The Pacific Ocean keeps the climate cool in summer, preventing much of the snow from melting. Here, glaciers are born by the thousands.

Glacial Geography

Alaska is an enormous land, with a varied landscape: rainy fjords, frigid tundra, vast river valleys, broad marshes and mountain ranges. Glaciers are found in nearly every region of this vast state.

Ruth Glacier – Denali National Park & Preserve

- High Arctic glaciers are rare, but there are a few in the eastern Brooks Range of northern Alaska.
- The Alaska Range, in the state's Interior, has many active glaciers—including some, such as Black Rapids and Susitna, that have been known to "surge" quickly forward.
- There are glaciers in the high volcanic peaks of the stormy, wind-swept Aleutian Islands. Some of the larger islands, such as Unimak and Unalaska, even have small icefields.

Mendenhall Glacier – Tongass National Forest

- Southcentral Alaska's Chugach Mountains hold one-third of all the state's glacier covered land—including the enormous Bering Glacier, the largest glacier in North America.
- On the Alaska Peninsula, active volcanoes and glaciers exist side by side. There are even some glaciers inside volcanic craters!
- Southeast Alaska has hundreds of glaciers, including the Mendenhall Glacier and the twelve tidewater glaciers of Glacier Bay National Park.

Unnamed Glacier – Chugach National Forest

2 Cirques and Piedmonts—Kinds of Glaciers

It's late summer, and you're riding in a small plane, flying from Anchorage over the Chugach Mountains. The rumble of the engine fills the little cabin, and you feel its vibration as you press your face against the cool plastic window.

The streets and houses of the city fall behind, until all you can see are green slopes and gray rocks. A grizzly bear shambles along a high ridge, and a handful of cream-colored Dall sheep graze in a south-facing meadow.

As the plane soars higher among the peaks, you begin to see patches of white among the peaks and valleys. Some of these patches are very small, while others cover entire slopes. Some look dirty, like melting snowbanks along a street in spring. Others are perfectly white. Some have deep cracks, in which you can see a blue glow.

Some of the white patches stretch down the centers of the high valleys, curving as the valleys turn. And ahead, even higher than your plane is flying, there's a smooth sheet of white surrounding a region of very tall, rugged peaks. Are some of those white patches glaciers? If so, which ones?

Glaciers come in many different sizes and shapes. Some are so huge that they engulf mountains; others are much smaller. Some are long and narrow, twisting like rivers, while others look more like frozen lakes.

Glacier Allstars

A ***hanging glacier*** is a glacier that spills from a high valley into a lower valley. Pieces of ice tumble down from it, onto the glacier or valley floor below.

The smallest glaciers form in hollows on mountain slopes. They have just enough ice to fill the "bowls" they're lying in, and to spill out of it a little. These are called ***cirque glaciers,*** after the French word for the circular mountain bowls they fill. A cirque glacier can be as small as a football stadium, but they are often much larger.

In some mountainous areas, such as the Coast, Wrangell, and St.Elias mountains, interwoven glaciers fill the high valleys, forming smooth plains of ice with a few peaks sticking out. These areas are called ***icefields.***

When a valley glacier spills out into the ocean, it's called a ***tidewater glacier.***

Sometimes a large valley glacier pours out of the mountains onto flat land, where the ice spreads out, like spilled milk, into a huge flat sheet. This is called a ***piedmont glacier*** (*piedmont* is French for "foot of the mountain").

Valley glaciers flow downhill between mountains, turning and bending around corners like rivers. Sometimes two or more small valley glaciers join together to make a larger valley glacier. A very large valley glacier can be made up of twenty or more smaller ones. One of the longest valley glaciers in Alaska is the valley section of the Bering Glacier, just east of Cordova. At over 100 miles, it's long enough to stretch from New York City to Philadelphia.

Anatomy of a Glacier

Just like an animal, a plant, or a river, a glacier has different parts. Scientists have come up with terms to describe those different parts.

1. The ***face*** is the very front of the glacier.
2. The glacier's downhill end is called its ***terminus.***
3. The top of the glacier is called its ***surface.***
4. The "belly" of the glacier (where it scrapes against the bottom of the valley) is called the ***base.***
5. The area from which the glacier flows is its ***source*** or ***head.***

Long Glacier – Wrangell-St. Elias National Park & Preserve

Pressure Melting

Activity

Glaciers flow around obstacles by a process called "pressure melting," where ice under pressure on the uphill side melts, then flows around to the downhill side and re-freezes. You can see this happen with the following investigation.

Freeze a milk carton full of water. Peel the milk carton off of the ice block and set the ice so that it makes a "bridge" between two tables, rocks, or railings, with at least two feet of space below. Tie heavy weights (about 3-5 pounds) to the ends of a 3-foot piece of wire (one weight at each end). Hang the wire across the ice block so the weights dangle on either side. Slowly, the wire will cut through the ice block—but when it has gone all the way through, the ice block should still be in one piece because the ice re-freezes behind the wire as it cuts through.

Takhinsha Mountains–west of Haines, AK

3
From Snow to Ice—How Glacier Ice Forms

You're standing in a high valley, in autumn. Below your feet is hard, grainy snow that has survived the warmth of summer. The air smells like frost. Cold wind pushes at the edges of your jacket and mittens, making you shiver. From the southeast, a snowstorm is approaching.

As the snow begins to fall, you lie down on your back to watch and listen. The snowflakes are as light and delicate as the down feathers inside your jacket. Each crystal is a lacy hexagon, so fragile that if you breathe on it, it will shrivel instantly into a miniscule waterdrop.

Glacier ice is not the same as the ice in an ice cube or the ice on a puddle or pond. It's formed from snow, not from liquid water.

The snowstorm thickens, until the snow has covered you in a soft blanket that's getting steadily heavier. The weight of the accumulating snow compresses your puffy jacket and ski pants, and you can feel it pressing on your arms, chest, and legs.

It's now almost silent beneath the snow layer, although you can hear soft sounds as the snow settles. You notice that you can no longer feel the wind's chill—your snow cover is keeping you insulated. You try lifting your arm—it's harder than you expected. The snow is so heavy even though it's made up of such tiny flakes!

You push upward, forcing your way through your thick snow shell, and emerge into the open air, where the moon skims the snow-dusted horizon. The storm has passed, but deep below you, glacier ice is being born.

Recipe for Glacier Ice

Ingredients: *Old snow, new snow, cold, time.*

Directions:

1. *In a large bowl of a high mountain valley, sprinkle new snow over old snow.*
2. *Add one year of time and a generous helping of cold, to keep the snow frozen.*
3. *Repeat 5 to 20 times*

Inside Mendenhall Glacier

Glacier ice is made of snow, cold, and time. It forms high in the mountains, where snow lingers through each summer, to be covered by more snow the following winter. As the snow builds up year after year, new snow layers weigh down on the old ones and keep them cold.

When it first falls, snow is full of air. But as more snow presses down upon it, air is forced out and flakes change from delicate crystals to tiny pellets. Gradually these pellets get pushed together, forming grainy ice called firn.

As the years go by and more snow falls above, the increased pressure pushes air out of the firn, and the firn crystals grow bigger. The little air that remains is squeezed into small bubbles. At last, the long-ago snowfall has been transformed into a layer of heavy, hard, clear ice. This is glacier ice.

How long does it take for snow to become glacier ice? That depends on temperature and amount of snow. Although cool temperatures are important for glacier ice to form, the process slows down if it's too cold. In the Chugach and Coast mountains, where temperatures are mild and there's lots of snow, it might take only four to six years for a layer of snow to turn to glacier ice. In the Alaska Range, where winters are very cold and not much snow falls, it may take much, much longer for this to happen.

How Glacier Ice Forms
New Fallen Snow
80% Air
Firn
(1 year)
50% Air
Glacier Ice
(4-15 years)
< 20% Air

Ice Formations

If you stand quietly near a piece of melting glacier ice, you'll hear it make snap! and pop! sounds. These are the sounds of pressurized air bubbles bursting as the ice melts.

As it flows and melts, glacier ice creates strange and beautiful sculptures.

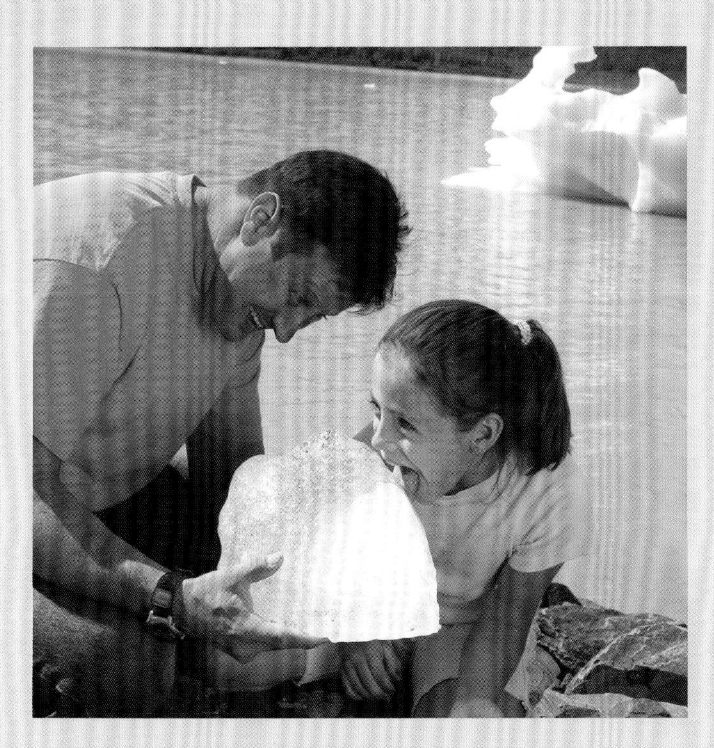

Have you ever kissed a glacier? One way to tell whether a piece of ice is firn or glacier ice is to suck on it. If you can suck water or air through it, it's firn. If you can't, it's glacier ice. Don't get your lips stuck!

Iceberg in a Glass

Activity

Glacier ice often has bubbles frozen inside. This is air that got trapped when the ice formed. Glacier bubbles are under such great pressure that when the ice melts they pop like tiny balloons. Although freezer ice is not exactly the same as glacier ice, you can see and hear similar bubbles in it.

Take an ice cube from your freezer and look closely at it. Most freezer cubes have many little bubbles trapped inside. Where are the bubbles—at the center, or on the outside?

What shapes are they? Put the cube into a clear glass half filled with warm water. Watch as the ice melts and the bubbles escape. Put your ear over the top of the glass. Can you hear the sizzling as the bubbles melt and rise to the surface?

Hubbard Glacier – Glacier Bay National Park & Preserve

4 Slumping and Sliding—How Glaciers Move

In the spring of 1986, Hubbard Glacier crept slowly across the mouth of Russell Fjord, near Yakutat. When the moving ice reached the opposite wall, it blocked the fjord entrance like a giant icy dam, trapping many seals and porpoises inside. Well-meaning people, worried about the trapped animals, tried hard to catch them so they could be released out in the ocean…but they couldn't catch a single seal or porpoise.

The glacier itself solved the dilemma—on October 8, the water that had been building up in the fjord burst through the ice dam in a massive flood, opening a passageway. The seals and porpoises swam out on their own. Maybe they, unlike some of the worried humans, understood that glaciers move and change, and chances were good that the Hubbard Glacier would eventually set them free.

Glaciers are almost never still. They're constantly shifting, breaking, flowing, melting, pushing, and pulling. They get longer or shorter, thicker or thinner. They bend around corners, break into crevasses, speed up and slow down. Hubbard Glacier has surged forward three times in the past twenty years—in 1986, in 2003, and again in 2005.

Creeping and Slipping

The massive weight of a glacier causes ice crystals deep inside to slide across each other, like playing cards in a tipped deck. They don't slide very far, but with millions of them slip-sliding away inside, the whole glacier slumps downhill, oozing its way along.

At the glacier's base, the ice presses and scrapes against rocks. This causes some of it to melt. The melted water forms a very slippery surface, on which the glacier slides downhill. In spring and summer, meltwater and rainwater trickle down through the glacier, where they help speed it up by keeping its rocky path slippery.

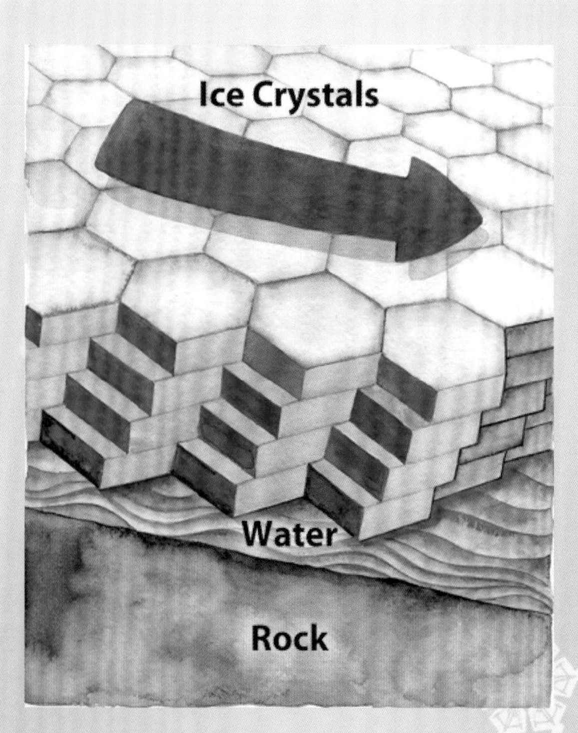

One important thing about glaciers is that they are always changing. They get longer or shorter, thicker or thinner. They bend around corners, break into crevasses, speed up and slow down. Glaciers are rivers of flowing ice.

Remember that glacier ice is formed from many layers of snow, building up over many years, until the bottom layers are squeezed into pure ice. But even after the snow turns into ice, it's not a glacier yet. To become a glacier, it has to start moving.

Imagine pouring thick cake batter onto a tilted cookie sheet. The batter would build up in a pile, but eventually it would start to flow and slide down the cookie sheet. This is a lot like the way a glacier begins. Snow builds up in a hollow on a mountainside, forming glacier ice. Gradually, the blue ice begins to spill down the slope. Once it starts moving, it's a glacier.

Speed

How fast does a glacier move? That depends on the temperature, the season, the location, and the shape of the glacier. Many glaciers flow faster in spring, when the ice begins to melt, and slower in fall and winter, when temperatures drop. Glaciers in cold, dry areas of Alaska such as the Alaska Range and the Brooks Range usually move slower than do glaciers on the coast. Thicker glaciers are usually speedier than thinner ones, and steeper glaciers are faster than ones on gentle slopes.

Regardless of their shape, location, or season, most Alaska glaciers move so slowly that you wouldn't be able to see them flow, even if you sat and watched them for a whole day. But if you plant a flag on a glacier, then come back a year later, your flag will have moved down toward the glacier's terminus, carried by the ice.

Not all parts of a glacier move at the same speed. Ice in the center moves faster than ice at the sides or the base, because the sides and base drag against the valley walls and floor, slowing them down. And ice moves faster where the glacier flows down a cliff or steep slope—kind of like water in a river speeding up as it goes down a waterfall.

Recession

Exit Glacier, near Seward, is now almost 2,000 feet shorter than it was in 1950. Mendenhall Glacier near Juneau has lost a mile in length since the 1940s. And the glaciers of Glacier Bay are now over 60 miles shorter than they were in the 1700s. When a glacier gets shorter, it's said to be retreating or receding.

Glaciers can't flow back uphill—so how can they retreat? At the top of the glacier where it's cold, ice is made, and at the bottom where it's warmer, ice melts away. Some of the melting ice is replaced by more ice flowing from above. But sometimes the melting is just too fast for the ice to be replaced, and the glacier gets shorter and shorter.

Snapping and Cracking

The ice at the base of a glacier, which is under great pressure from the weight of the ice above, bends as it flows over the ground. But the ice in the top 100 feet or so is more brittle. When the ice below flows over a bump, or when one part of the glacier is moving faster than another part, the top layer of ice snaps, and big cracks called crevasses open up.

Mendenhall Glacier – Tongass National Forest

Race the Face

Who would win a footrace: you, or a surging glacier? Well, unless you got too close and got squished by a falling piece of ice, you'd probably win. Even though glaciers are pushing forward much faster than their "normal" speed, most "galloping" glaciers still move slower than a crawling slug.

Exit Glacier – Kenai Fjords National Park

Galloping Glaciers

Sometimes, a glacier will leap into fast motion, rushing forward at up to ten times its "normal" speed. It'll shove its way down its valley, bulldozing hills and crushing trees...then abruptly slow back down to normal. This is called surging.

What makes a glacier surge? Scientists still aren't totally sure, but from measurements on and in the ice of surging glaciers, they think it may happen when water (from melting and other sources) builds up underneath and lifts part of the glacier up, allowing it to "float" and move more quickly downvalley. Afterward, the water drains out and the glacier settles back onto to its bed, slowing down.

Scientists do know that certain glaciers have a history of many surges. They've even been able to predict surges, based on measurements of these glaciers' flow.

Right: In the winter of 1936/1937, the Black Rapids Glacier in the Alaska Range gave the Revell family quite a scare. For three months, the glacier (which had been receding for many years) surged forward almost four miles, bearing down on the Revells' home and business, the Black Rapids Roadhouse. Fortunately, the glacier stopped before it reached their house.

Glacial Erractics – Denali National Park & Preserve

5 Breaking and Building—How Glaciers Shape the Land

The boulder is enormous—the size of a small house. It's blocky, with rounded corners, and as speckled as a bird's egg. It seems very out of place on this smooth slope of tundra. As you approach, you hear a sharp "sik-sik!" alarm call, and watch an arctic ground squirrel dive into a den entrance under the boulder's edge.

You find a low place on one side and scramble up to the rock's summit, where lichens cling to the rough stone. By standing on tiptoe and peering far up a valley to the north, you can just catch a glimpse of the face of a glacier, gleaming white, with tall mountain peaks rising behind it.

The boulder came from those high peaks. But how did it get all the way down here?

As they flow across the land, glaciers pick up, carry, and push millions of tons of debris—from tiny grains of silt to enormous boulders. When they melt away, they leave that debris behind.

Glacier Stripes

It's easy to see till on many valley glaciers. Look for dark stripes at the edges of the ice where the glacier scrapes against the valley walls. These lateral moraines are made up of till the glacier has collected.

When two glaciers flow together, their lateral moraines get sandwiched between, creating a single dark stripe called a medial moraine. Some Alaska glaciers have twenty or more medial moraines, showing that they are made up of at least twenty smaller glaciers joining together.

Kennicott Glacier – Wrangel-St. Elias National Park & Preserve

There aren't many forces in nature more powerful than glaciers. They sharpen mountain peaks, scoop out valleys, carve and smooth cliffs, build hills and ponds and lakes. They carry stones from the mountains to the sea. They give birth to rivers that carve and shape the land even further.

Carving

If you scrape an ice cube against a piece of rock, it's the ice that'll give way, not the rock. As you rub, the ice will melt and disappear, and if you keep it up, all you'll have left is a wet rock...and cold hands. So how can glaciers (just giant pieces of ice, after all) wear down mountains? With their own homemade sandpaper.

At the base of the glacier, rocks get plucked (picked up) by the moving ice. This happens when the ice slides over loose rocks, which freeze to the glacier's base (like your tongue sticking to a cold icicle). Plucking also happens when meltwater trickles into cracks in the rocks, freezes, and pushes outward. The force of the expanding ice breaks chunks of rock loose, and they stick to the bottom of the glacier as well.

Now imagine dipping an ice cube in sand, and then rubbing it against a rock. This time, your ice cube would still melt as you rubbed, but the sand would leave scratches in the rock. If you did it long enough, with enough ice cubes and sand, you could smooth the rock.

That's how glaciers carve mountains: as they travel downhill, the rock and sand layer on their bellies scrapes and grinds away the rocks below. It takes thousands of years, but they can eventually carve valleys hundreds or thousands of feet deep.

Building

What happens to a glacier's rock collection? It gets carried downhill until the ice melts out from around it. The glacier acts like a giant conveyor belt, carrying rocks from the mountains to the lowlands.

The load of rocks and sand carried in and on a glacier is what scientists call till. The piles of till on the glacier, and the piles the glacier leaves behind, are called moraines.

Rivers

Every glacier has at least one meltwater river flowing from it. These rivers are usually very cold, and milky from a kind of dust called glacial flour or glacial silt. Just like the dust you create when you rub two rocks together, the silt is formed when the glacier scrapes its rocky base over bedrock. Then the silt is washed out from under the glacier by meltwater.

Because they change course as the glacier advances or retreats, glacial rivers move back and forth across the glacier's valley, shifting the till. The area they flow over is called the glacier's outwash plain.

Handheld Glaciers

Activity

Glaciers slide downhill on a layer of slippery meltwater. They carve bedrock by scraping other rocks against it. You can experiment with these ideas by making "handheld glaciers."

Put about a teaspoon of sand and pebbles in the bottom of each of three small paper cups, and then fill the cups halfway with water. Put the cups in the freezer. When the water has frozen, peel the cups from the ice. You should have three chunks of ice with sand frozen to the bottoms.

Find a flat, soft rock (shale and slate are good choices; look on riverbanks or by the beach). Try rubbing the top (sand-free end) of your "glacier" against the rock (wear gloves to keep your hands warm). As you rub, the ice should melt and get slipperier.

Turn the "glacier" over and rub the sandy end against the rock. What does this feel like? After you've scraped for a while, wipe the water and sand off the rock and look closely. Can you see striations (scrape marks)? Experiment with different kinds of rock to see which ones scratch the easiest.

Make Kettle Ponds

Activity

Kettle ponds are formed when big chunks of ice melt away and leave pits in the glacier's outwash plain. Take some ice cubes to a sandbox, beach, or other sandy area. Bury the cubes in the sand (some halfway, others most of the way). Check back over time as the ice cubes melt. They should leave behind tiny pits in the sand. To make "kettle ponds" that have water in them, use clay instead of sand.

Nizina Glacier, Wrangell-St. Elias National Park & Preserve

Glacier Features

Carved:

1. ***Glacial valleys*** are broad and flat-bottomed, shaped like the letter "U."
2. Bowl-shaped areas carved out of mountainsides are called ***cirques.***
3. Cirque glaciers wearing away the sides of mountain peaks carve sharp pointed peaks, called ***horns.***
4. Two glaciers flowing side by side carve a knife-edged ridge between them called an ***arête.***
5. Grooves carved in bedrock are called ***striations.***

Deposited:

6. ***Terminal moraines*** are big piles of rock left by the glacier's terminus.
7. Where big blocks of ice sat buried in till then melted away, ***kettle ponds*** form.
8. ***Kames*** are little hills of till that formed inside the glacier, and then got left behind.

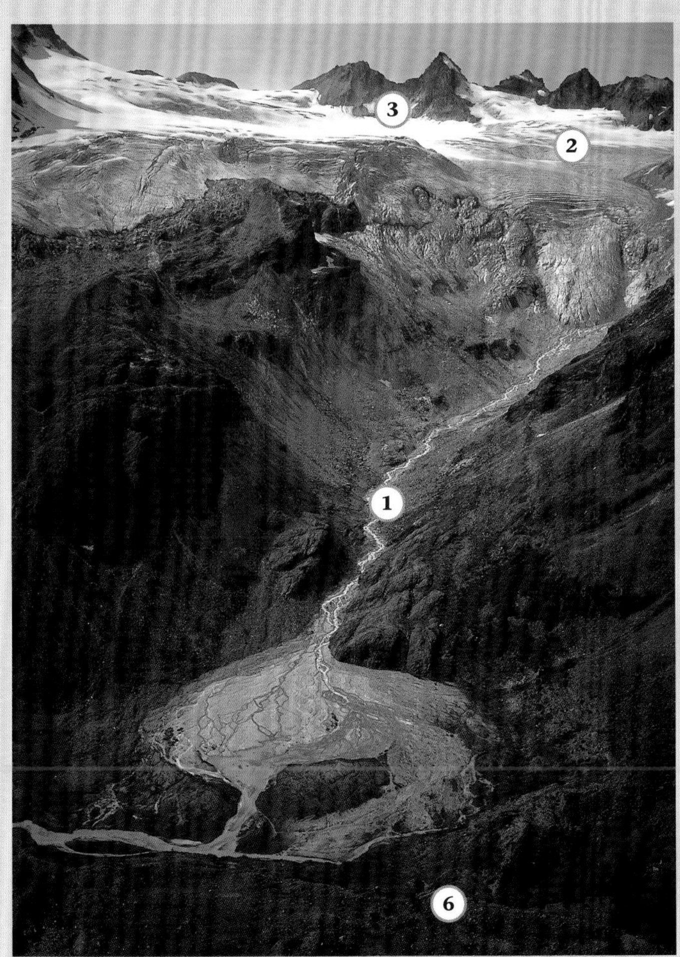

Denali National Park & Preserve

Wrangell-St. Elias National Park & Preserve

Tongass Natinal Forest

Kenai Fjords National Park

Pedersen Glacier – Kenai Fjords National Park

6 Life on Ice—Plants and Animals of Glacier Country

For half an hour you've been hiking across the smooth, bald bedrock at the face of the melting glacier. It's June, and there's a light rain falling. You've been keeping your head down to watch for slippery spots. The ground under your feet is almost completely barren—only lichens and sparse patches of tough-looking plants cling to the rocks and the sandy soil.

Suddenly, out of the corner of your eye, you catch a flash of color, bright against the cold gray rocks. You stop to investigate. To your surprise and delight, it's a flowering plant—dwarf fireweed—opening vivid blossoms to greet the spring.

Only a few years ago, the glacier covered this spot. But as the ice melts, life follows, creeping across the cold, raw ground.

A glacier's gift to the living world is brand-new land, open and waiting for plants and animals to move in.

A Glacial Forest

These dead trees were a part of a forest that was crushed by a glacier many centuries ago. The glacier then retreated, exposing the old stumps.

Near several Alaska glaciers you can find stumps and trunks of long-dead trees, buried under layers of new glacial till. These trees are the remains of forests destroyed by advancing glaciers. When the glaciers receded, they dumped till on the dead trees. These "fossil" forests come to light again when rivers cut through the till.

Glacier Bay National Park & Preserve

When a glacier flows over an area, it destroys all life in its path. It crushes forests, and buries meadows, lakes, and wetlands under ice and debris. Nothing can survive being buried under an advancing glacier.

But when the glacier melts away, it leaves behind a whole new world of hills, valleys, cliffs, plains, rivers, and lakes, open and waiting for plants and animals to move in.

Mosses, lichens, and small plants such as fireweed and lupine are usually the first things to grow in the new soil that a glacier leaves behind. Soon afterward, trees such as willow, cottonwood, birch, and spruce arrive, their seeds blown in on the wind. Thickets and forests grow. Gradually, dead leaves and fallen branches rot, making the soil richer.

Animals move into the new world, following the plants. Insects eat the plants and drink the nectar from the flowers. Birds such as plovers, sparrows, and warblers nest in the moss and lichen, or among the branches of the trees and shrubs.

Plant-eating mammals such as moose move in to browse on willow, followed by predators such as wolves (to browse on moose!). Fish find their way up the new creeks and rivers. Gradually, life in the area grows richer...

...Until the glacier advances again, starting things over.

Animals on Ice

Although wolves, bears, and other large animals will sometimes travel across glaciers, most animals don't linger on the ice. It's too cold, and there's very little to eat. However, a couple of Alaska animals actually use glaciers to help them survive.

In Southeast and Southcentral Alaska, pregnant harbor seals migrate to tidewater glaciers, where they climb up on the icebergs to give birth and nurse their pups. This helps keep the pups protected from predators such as bears.

Iceworms are very small worms found on many Alaska glaciers. They're related to earthworms and night crawlers. Iceworms actually live in the ice, burrowing deeper when the sun is out (does that mean they're the "coolest" Alaska animals?) They dine on algae—microscopic plants that grow in the ice—spiced with dashes of windblown pollen.

Some high-mountain birds, such as American pipits, go to the glacier for lunch and pick ice-killed insects from the ice surface.

Glacier Bay National Park & Preserve

Right: A mother harbor seal and her pup rest on their icy cradle.

Bering Land Bridge – National Preserve

7 Ancient Ice—Glaciers in Alaska's Past

The arctic sun is low in the sky, but it's still warm on your shoulders, and the mosquitoes are whining in your ears. You're on a river trip, canoeing in the Koyukuk River country north of Fairbanks. You've just paddled your canoe around a bend in the river when your guide calls from ahead: "Come look at this!" You paddle over.

Alaska's Interior was once a sweep of steppe (grassland), hemmed on the north and the south by glacier ice. Across this grassland roamed prehistoric animals such as mammoths, bison, and saber-toothed cats.

The guide is pointing to a spot where the stream has cut into the frozen soil, creating a steep, crumbling bank. Something is sticking out. At first you think it might be just a tree root, but when you look closer, you can see it's actually a smooth pale tusk! Nearby, tufts of reddish-brown hair are melting out of the frozen soil.

The guide smiles. "It's a mammoth. They went extinct in Alaska just after the last Ice Age."

"How long has it been here?" you ask.

"Probably about fifteen thousand years," he replies.

13,000-10,000 years ago

Earth's climate got warmer, and the great ice age glaciers melted back, leaving jagged mountains and U-shaped valleys. The rising ocean covered the land between Alaska and Siberia, and the ice-free areas along the southern coast. Forests of spruce and birch replaced the grasslands in the center of Alaska. Mammoths, horses, and other animals that depended on the grasslands died out.

24,000-13,000 years ago

Earth's climate was much colder than it is today, and glaciers covered one quarter of our planet's dry land. This period is called the Wisconsin Ice Age. At the height of this age, about half of Alaska was buried under glacier ice. The rest of Alaska's land was dry, cold tundra and grassland. Mammoths, saber-toothed cats, ancient horses, and other prehistoric animals roamed the ice-free region between the Alaska Range and the Brooks Range.

Because so much of the Earth's water was frozen into the ice age glaciers, sea levels were much lower than they are now, and the sea floor between what's now Alaska and what's now Siberia was dry land. There were ice-free areas along Alaska's southern coast as well, where bears, caribou, lemmings, saiga antelope, and other tundra animals lived.

Long-ago humans, whose ancestors had come from Asia, lived on the land "bridge" between North America and Asia, and some of their descendents traveled east and south to become the first people of North America.

10,000 years ago

Alaska looked much like it does today: the glaciers were about the same size as they are now, and the same kinds of plants and animals lived here.

-24,000 -13,000 -10,000

Harding Icefield – Kenai Fjords National Park
300 years ago to the present
The Little Ice Age ended as temperatures rose. Alaska's glaciers (and those in the rest of North America, as well as Europe, Asia, Canada, South America, Africa, Antarctica, and New Zealand) melted back. Many are still melting today.
650 years ago
Around the world, the climate got cooler. Glaciers grew much bigger-though they did not get as big as they had during the Wisconsin Ice Age. This period is called the Little Ice Age.
10,000-1,000 years ago
Alaska's climate shifted several times from cooler to warmer, and back to cooler. Glaciers grew and shrunk, as temperatures changed.
-1,000
-650
-300

Tracks of the Past

Kenai Fjords National Park

Scientists use many clues to figure out Alaska's glacial history. Pollen samples, taken from the bottoms of lakes and ponds, reveal what plants grew in Alaska as the climate changed over the millennia.

The shapes of mountains and valleys show where glaciers were thousands of years ago.

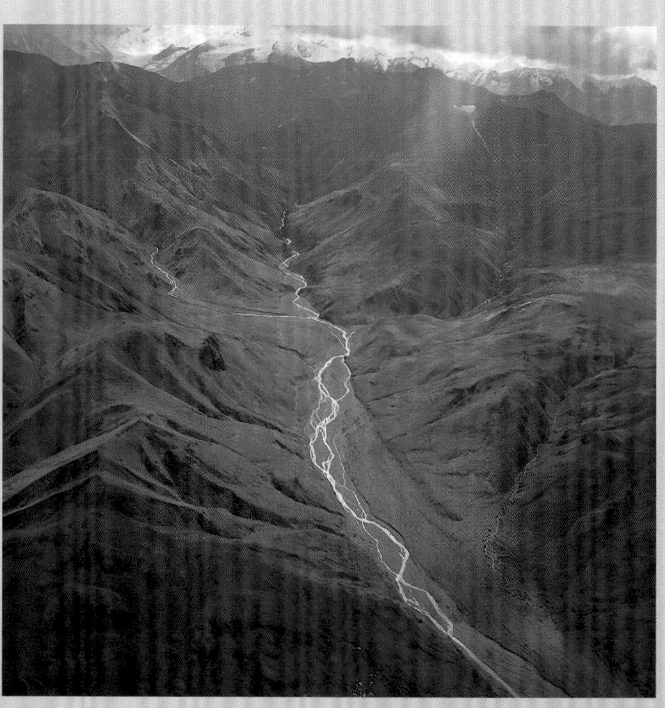

Denali National Park

Denali National Park

Moraines, erratics, eskers, and patterns of old river channels allow researchers to reconstruct where ancient glaciers once flowed and melted.

Changing Tides

During the last ice age, the weight of glacier ice pushed down on some regions of Alaska so much that the land sank downward. As the glaciers melted away, the land rose like an unloaded boat.

Today, you can find evidence of that earth movement high on some of Alaska's coastal mountainsides. In places once covered by the ocean, marine-deposited clay—sometimes mixed with fossil shells—now lies on dry land.

Above: These 9,000-12,000 year old shells came from ancient ocean deposits on a hillside near Juneau.

Juneau Icefield – Tongass National Forest

8

What's Next?—Glaciers and the Future

The crunch of shovels in snow is the only sound you can hear— here are no birdcalls, no car noises. You scoop another shovelfull up out of the snow pit, and then pause to wipe the sweat off your face and look around. For miles, all you can see is smooth snow and sharp mountain peaks, under a deep blue sky. The sun's glare on the snow is fierce—you put your sunglasses back on, and go back to digging.

You're up on the Juneau Icefield, studying the Mendenhall Glacier with scientists from the University of Alaska Geophysical Institute. Today, you're helping dig a pit to measure how much of last winter's snow has remained through this summer. The thickness of that layer will determine how much ice the glacier can make.

Pushing your shovel blade into the soft snow underfoot, you strike a harder surface. Your partner comes over to help you dig, clearing away the snow from a layer of hard, grainy ice. "There it is," she says, "Last year's summer surface." She points to the thickness of snow you've dug through and shakes her head. "There has been less and less snow accumulating up here each year. That's why the glacier is shrinking."

Glacier researchers have to be ready for all kinds of weather. On a glacier, it can be bitter cold, wet and miserable, balmy and springlike... or hot and sunny!

Blue Light

If you are lucky enough to get a close look at a large iceberg, or at the inside of a glacier crevasse, you'll be impressed at its rich blue color. Lake ice, river ice, and ice cubes are all clear, or white. Why is glacier ice blue?

Light is made up of many colors, all blended together. When light strikes or passes through an object, some of its colors are absorbed and others pass through. What colors are absorbed depend on what the object is made of. If it's thick enough, glacier ice absorbs red and yellow light, leaving only blue light for us to see. Thinner pieces are clear.

Mendenhall Glacier, Tongass National Forest

Glaciers are important to us for many reasons. Is your home in a mountain valley? A glacier probably carved the ground underneath you. Did you eat cereal or toast for breakfast? The wheat or oats you munched were probably grown in soil that was deposited by glaciers. Glaciers hold over three-quarters of all the fresh water in the world. If Earth's glaciers all melted tomorrow, oceans would rise over 250 feet.

Alaska, with its thousands of accessible and active glaciers, is an important site for glacier research. So what are scientists finding out about Alaska glaciers? They've found that glaciers hold clues to Alaska's history, such as layers of ash from long-ago volcanoes. They've discovered that some areas of the state (such as northern Southeast Alaska) are actually rising in elevation as glaciers melt and the weight of the ice disappears. One of the big discoveries that glaciologists have made is that most glaciers in Alaska have been getting smaller. Some glaciers have completely disappeared. Why?—Because our planet's climate is getting warmer, especially in northern regions such as Alaska. This means more rain and less snow, and faster melting.

But even if Alaska's glaciers continue to melt, it would be a very long time before all of them disappeared. It's also possible that they'll begin to grow again. Regardless, glaciers will remain an important part of Alaska's landscape for our foreseeable future.

Juneau Icefield – Tongass National Forest

Skis and Satellites, Crampons and Computers

Glaciologists use both high technology and old-fashioned elbow grease to study Alaska's glaciers. Here are a few of the tools they use:

***GPS (Global Positioning System) Devices*—** Researchers use these handheld computers, which calculate precise locations on Earth's surface using satellite readings, to make maps of glacier shapes. Maps from each year can be compared to see how each glacier's shape is changing.

***Laser Altimeter*—** A scientist flying in a small plane can use this instrument to create a very detailed map of a glacier's surface. It's much faster than walking or skiing across the ice to take measurements!

***Radar or Seismic Sensing*—** Glaciologists send electromagnetic or pressure pulses down through the glacier. The pulses echo off the rock underneath, and instruments record the echoes and calculate how thick the glacier is.

***Shovel and ice axe*—**These are still some of the most important tools for studying glaciers. Glaciologists use shovels and ice axes to dig snow pits at the top of the glacier, studying the layers of ice and firn.

Probes — These are long poles, usually made of aluminum or another metal. Researchers stick them down into the glacier's surface, then measure where the ice comes to at the beginning and the end of the summer. This tells them how much has melted from the surface.

Cameras — Some scientists study old photos of glaciers and compare them with modern photos from the same places. This helps them measure how the glaciers have changed. Others compare old and new satellite images.

Glacier Science

Because glaciers are such an important part of our planet, scientists have been studying them for over a hundred years. Glaciologists measure glacier speeds and depths, and the rates at which they form ice, erode the land, and melt. They try to predict how fast glaciers will advance or recede, and to understand how glaciers shape the land.

Exit Glacier–Kenai Fjords National Park

Glossary

Accumulation	The buildup of snow over several years. (pg. 10)
Advance	The forward motion of a glacier's terminus. (pg. 51)
Arête	A sharp-edged mountain ridge that divides two glacial valleys. (pg. 34)
Base	The part of a glacier that touches the ground below. (pg. 16,26,27,32,33)
Bedrock	Solid rock that lies underneath the soil. (pg. 33,34,37)
Cirque/ cirque glacier	Cirque: an ice-carved, bowl-shaped depression on a mountainside, usually in the upper reaches of a mountain valley. Cirque glacier: a glacier that has formed inside a cirque. (pg. 14,34)
Climate	The pattern of temperature, rainfall, and wind, averaged over time. (pg. 5,10,42,43,44,48)
Compress	To squeeze together under pressure.
Crevasse	A crack in a glacier's surface. (pg. 7,25,26,27,48)
Erratic	A boulder that has been carried from its source and deposited by a glacier. (pg. 45)
Esker	A twisty ridge of sand and rock, formed by a stream running underneath or within a glacier, between ice walls or in an ice tunnel. (pg. 45)
Firn	Grainy ice–formed from snow-that is on its way to becoming glacier ice. (pg. 20,21,23,50)
Fjord	A long, deep arm of the ocean, carved out by a glacier. (pg. 11,25)
Glacial flour/ glacial silt	Fine rock powder formed when the glacier rubs rocks together or against bedrock. (pg. 33)

Glacial deformation	Glacier flow caused by ice crystals sliding over each other.
Glacial recession	When a glacier's terminus melts away faster than it is being pushed forward. (pg. 27)
Glacial retreat	When a glacier's terminus melts away faster than it is being pushed forward. (pg. 27)
Glacier Face	The front of the glacier. (pg. 8,10,16,31)
Glaciologist	A scientist who studies glaciers. (pg. 48, 50, 51)
Hanging glacier	A glacier that spills from a high valley into a lower valley. (pg. 14)
Head	The upper part of the glacier, where ice is formed. (pg. 16)
Horn	A sharp mountain peak formed when three or more glaciers carve out converging cirques. (pg. 34)
Ice Age	A cold period in Earth's history, when glaciers advance. (pg. 41,42,43,45)
Iceberg	A large piece of floating ice that has broken away from a glacier. (pg. 23,48)
Icefield	An area of glacial ice covering a large expanse of land among high mountain peaks. (pg. 10,11,14,47)
Kame	A small hill of rocks and sand formed inside a glacier and then left behind. (pg. 35)
Kettle pond	A pond left behind when a large iceberg melts, leaving a water-filled hollow. (pg. 34,35)
Meltwater	Water that melts from glacial ice. (pg. 26,32,33)
Moraine	A pile of sand, gravel, cobbles, and boulders that a glacier has collected. (pg. 8,32)

Moraine (lateral, medial, terminal)	**Lateral:** a moraine along the side of the glacier, made up of rocks falling from the valley walls or scraped from the sides. **Medial:** a moraine in the center of the glacier, formed when two glaciers flow together. **Terminal:** a moraine deposited at the face of a glacier.
Nunatak	An isolated mountain peak surrounded by a "sea" of glacier ice.
Outwash plain	An area in front of a glacier where glacial till is shaped by meltwater rivers and streams. (pg. 33,34)
Piedmont glacier	A huge lobe of glacier ice that has spilled out of the mountains and across a flat plain. (pg. 15)
Plucking	When the base of a glacier picks up rocks as it moves over bedrock. (pg. 32)
Snow pit	A hole dug in the snow on top of a glacier to study the layers within. (pg. 47)
Source	The upper part of the glacier, where ice is formed. (pg. 16)
Striations	Scratches in the bedrock caused by a glacier scraping other rocks against it. (pg. 33,34)
Surface	The top of the glacier, where it's exposed to sun, wind, and rain. (pg. 7,8,16,23,26,39,50)
Surge	When a glacier suddenly flows forward much faster than normal. (pg. 11,28)
Terminus	The lower end of the glacier. (pg. 16,27,34)
Tidewater glacier	A glacier whose terminus is in the ocean. (pg. 14)
Till	Sand, gravel, and rocks carried and left behind by a glacier. (pg. 32,33,34,38)
Tundra	A treeless, cold, dry habitat with lichens, mosses, grasses, and low shrubs. (pg. 11,31,42)
Valley glacier	A glacier that flows down a valley. (pg. 15)